Ethics in Action Empow

in Bus

Helena

Copyright © [2023]

Title: Ethics in Action Empowering Every Individual in Business

Author's: Helena.

All rights reserved. No part of this publication may be reproduced, stored in a retrieval system, or transmitted in any form or by any means, electronic, mechanical, photocopying, recording, or otherwise, without the prior written permission of the publisher or author, except in the case of brief quotations embodied in critical reviews and certain other non-commercial uses permitted by copyright law.

This book was printed and published by [Publisher's: Helena] in [2023]

ISBN:

TABLE OF CONTENTS

Chapter 1: Introduction to Ethical Decision-Making in Business 07

Understanding the Importance of Ethics in Business

The Impact of Ethical Decision-Making on Individuals and Organizations

Overview of Ethical Theories and Frameworks

Chapter 2: Ethical Leadership and its Role in Empowering Individuals 13

The Characteristics of Ethical Leaders

The Influence of Ethical Leadership on Employee Morale and Motivation

Empowering Individuals through Ethical Leadership Practices

Chapter 3: Creating an Ethical Organizational Culture 19

Developing and Communicating Ethical Values and Standards

Implementing Ethical Codes of Conduct

Fostering Ethical Decision-Making through Organizational Policies and Procedures

Chapter 4: Ethical Decision-Making Models and Approaches 25

The Utilitarian Approach

The Deontological Approach

The Virtue Ethics Approach

Integrating Multiple Approaches for Ethical Decision-Making

Chapter 5: Identifying Ethical Dilemmas in Business 33

Recognizing Ethical Issues and Challenges

Understanding the Factors that Contribute to Ethical Dilemmas

Ethical Decision-Making in Complex Situations

Chapter 6: Strategies for Resolving Ethical Dilemmas 40

Analyzing the Consequences and Implications

Considering Stakeholder Perspectives

Seeking Guidance from Ethical Experts or Professionals

Ethical Decision-Making in Group Settings

Chapter 7: Ethical Communication and Transparency in Business 48

The Role of Open and Honest Communication in Ethical Decision-Making

Building Trust and Credibility through Transparent Practices

Addressing Ethical Concerns and Whistleblowing

Chapter 8: Ethical Leadership and the Bottom Line 54

The Relationship between Ethical Leadership and Organizational Performance

The Long-Term Benefits of Ethical Decision-Making

Overcoming Challenges and Resistance to Ethical Practices

Chapter 9: Implementing Ethical Decision-Making in Business 60

Developing an Ethical Decision-Making Framework

Training and Educating Employees on Ethical Practices

Evaluating and Monitoring Ethical Performance

Chapter 10: Conclusion: Empowering Every Individual in Business 66

Recap of Key Concepts and Insights

The Ongoing Journey of Ethical Decision-Making

Inspiring a Culture of Ethical Responsibility and Empowerment

Chapter 1: Introduction to Ethical Decision-Making in Business

Understanding the Importance of Ethics in Business

In today's fast-paced and competitive business world, it is crucial to recognize and understand the importance of ethics. Ethics plays a significant role in shaping the culture, values, and overall success of any organization. In this subchapter, we will delve into the fundamental aspects of business ethics and highlight how it empowers individuals in the corporate world.

Business ethics refers to the moral principles and values that guide the behavior and decision-making process within an organization. It involves conducting business in an honest, fair, and transparent manner, while considering the impact on various stakeholders, such as employees, customers, suppliers, and the community at large.

One of the key reasons why ethics is vital in business is its ability to build trust. When organizations operate ethically, they create a positive reputation and establish trust among their stakeholders. This trust, in turn, leads to stronger relationships, increased customer loyalty, and enhanced brand reputation. A strong ethical foundation also attracts and retains top talent, as employees are more likely to work for organizations that align with their personal values.

Ethics in business also fosters a culture of accountability. By adhering to ethical standards, individuals within the organization are held responsible for their actions. This accountability ensures that everyone is working towards the same ethical goals and objectives, promoting fairness and equality in the workplace. Moreover, when organizations prioritize ethics, it becomes easier to identify and address unethical behavior promptly, preventing potential legal and reputational risks.

Furthermore, business ethics enables organizations to make socially responsible decisions. In today's globalized world, companies are increasingly expected to consider the impact of their actions on society and the environment. Ethical business practices ensure that organizations operate in a sustainable manner, minimizing harm to the environment, promoting diversity and inclusion, and giving back to the community through various corporate social responsibility initiatives.

In conclusion, understanding the importance of ethics in business is essential for every individual involved in the corporate world. By prioritizing ethics, organizations can build trust, foster accountability, and make socially responsible decisions. Embracing a strong ethical foundation empowers individuals to make principled choices, leading to long-term success, both for the organization and the society it operates in.

The Impact of Ethical Decision-Making on Individuals and Organizations

Ethics form the backbone of any successful organization, shaping its culture, reputation, and overall performance. In today's complex business landscape, ethical decision-making plays a pivotal role in determining the long-term sustainability and growth of both individuals and organizations. This subchapter explores the profound impact ethical decision-making has on individuals and organizations, shedding light on its significance in the realm of business ethics.

At an individual level, ethical decision-making is instrumental in shaping one's character and personal growth. When individuals consistently make ethical choices, they cultivate a sense of integrity, empathy, and accountability. These qualities not only enhance their own self-image but also contribute to a positive work environment and fruitful relationships. Ethical individuals are respected and trusted by their colleagues, clients, and superiors, which opens doors to new opportunities and fosters career progression.

Moreover, ethical decision-making has a ripple effect on organizations as a whole. When leaders prioritize ethics and encourage their employees to do the same, it creates an ethical culture within the organization. This culture sets the foundation for trust, loyalty, and commitment among employees, leading to increased job satisfaction and productivity. Ethical organizations are more likely to attract and retain top talent, as individuals seek environments that align with their personal values.

Additionally, ethical decision-making safeguards an organization's reputation and mitigates risks. By adhering to ethical principles, organizations demonstrate their commitment to acting in the best interests of their stakeholders, including customers, investors, and the community at large. This builds trust and credibility, positioning the organization as a responsible corporate citizen. In contrast, unethical behavior can severely damage an organization's reputation, resulting in financial and legal repercussions.

Furthermore, ethical decision-making enables organizations to navigate complex ethical dilemmas and make sound judgments. By considering the ethical implications of their actions, organizations can avoid costly mistakes and make decisions that align with their values and long-term goals. This ultimately leads to sustainable growth and success.

In conclusion, ethical decision-making has a profound impact on both individuals and organizations in the realm of business ethics. It shapes individual character, fosters a positive work environment, and enhances career prospects. At the organizational level, ethical decision-making establishes a culture of trust, attracts top talent, safeguards reputation, and enables sound judgment. Embracing ethical decision-making is not only the right thing to do but also a strategic imperative for every individual and organization striving for success in today's business landscape.

Overview of Ethical Theories and Frameworks

In the world of business ethics, it is crucial to have a solid understanding of ethical theories and frameworks that guide ethical decision-making. These theories and frameworks provide individuals with a set of principles and guidelines to navigate complex ethical dilemmas that arise in the business world. In this subchapter, we will explore the various ethical theories and frameworks that can empower every individual in business to make ethical choices.

One of the most prominent ethical theories is consequentialism, which focuses on the outcomes or consequences of one's actions. According to consequentialism, an action is considered ethically right if it leads to the greatest amount of overall happiness or the least amount of harm. This theory often involves calculating the potential consequences and weighing the benefits against the potential harm.

Another important ethical theory is deontology, which emphasizes the moral duty or obligation individuals have to follow certain rules or principles. Deontological ethics suggest that actions are inherently right or wrong, regardless of their consequences. It encourages individuals to act in accordance with universally applicable principles, such as honesty, fairness, and respect.

Furthermore, virtue ethics is a framework that emphasizes the development of moral character and virtues. It focuses on the traits and qualities that individuals should possess to make ethical decisions consistently. Virtue ethics encourages individuals to cultivate virtues such as honesty, integrity, and compassion, which ultimately guide their actions and decision-making.

In addition to these ethical theories, there are various frameworks that can assist individuals in making ethical decisions. The ethical decision-making process often involves steps such as identifying the problem, gathering information, evaluating alternatives, and making a choice based on ethical principles. Frameworks like the Four-Way Test, Ethical Decision-Making Model, and the Universal Ethical Principles Framework provide individuals with a structured approach to ethical decision-making.

Understanding these ethical theories and frameworks is essential for every individual in business, as it enables them to navigate the ethical complexities they may encounter. By having a solid grasp of these principles, individuals can make informed decisions that align with their personal values and the ethical standards of the organization they work for.

In conclusion, this subchapter provides an overview of ethical theories and frameworks that empower every individual in business to make ethical choices. By understanding consequentialism, deontology, virtue ethics, and various ethical decision-making frameworks, individuals can navigate ethical dilemmas with confidence and integrity. These theories and frameworks serve as invaluable tools for creating a culture of ethics in business, ensuring that ethical decision-making becomes an integral part of every individual's professional journey.

Chapter 2: Ethical Leadership and its Role in Empowering Individuals

The Characteristics of Ethical Leaders

In the world of business, ethical leadership is paramount to ensuring the success and sustainability of organizations. Ethical leaders set the tone for their teams and create an environment built on trust, integrity, and fairness. They understand that their actions and decisions have a profound impact on their employees, customers, and society as a whole. In this subchapter, we will explore the key characteristics that define ethical leaders and why they are essential in today's business landscape.

First and foremost, ethical leaders possess a strong sense of moral character. They adhere to a set of principles and values that guide their behavior and decision-making processes. These leaders consistently demonstrate honesty, transparency, and accountability, earning the respect and trust of their followers. Their actions align with their words, and they are willing to take responsibility for any mistakes or failures that may occur.

Furthermore, ethical leaders are empathetic and compassionate. They understand the importance of treating others with dignity and respect, valuing diverse perspectives, and fostering a culture of inclusivity. By actively listening and understanding the needs and concerns of their employees, they create an environment where everyone feels heard and valued. This, in turn, leads to higher employee engagement and productivity.

Ethical leaders also possess excellent communication skills. They are able to clearly articulate their vision, values, and expectations, ensuring that everyone in the organization understands and aligns with them. They actively encourage open and honest dialogue, promoting a culture of transparency and collaboration. By effectively communicating their ethical standards, they inspire their teams to make principled decisions and act in the best interest of all stakeholders.

Moreover, ethical leaders lead by example. They not only talk about ethical behavior but also demonstrate it through their actions. They make ethical decisions even when faced with difficult choices, prioritizing long-term benefits over short-term gains. By consistently modeling ethical behavior, they create a culture of integrity and inspire others to follow suit.

In conclusion, ethical leaders possess a unique set of qualities that set them apart in the business world. They have a strong moral character, are empathetic and compassionate, possess excellent communication skills, and lead by example. These characteristics are crucial in fostering an ethical organizational culture and ensuring the long-term success of businesses. By embodying these qualities, leaders can empower every individual in business to act ethically and make a positive impact on society as a whole.

The Influence of Ethical Leadership on Employee Morale and Motivation

In today's fast-paced and competitive business world, the role of ethical leadership cannot be underestimated. Ethical leaders inspire their employees to strive for excellence, foster a positive work environment, and ultimately drive the success of the organization. This subchapter explores the significant impact that ethical leadership has on employee morale and motivation, shedding light on how it can empower individuals in the realm of business ethics.

Ethical leaders are individuals who not only prioritize organizational goals but also place a strong emphasis on ethical behavior. They lead by example, demonstrating integrity, fairness, and a genuine concern for the well-being of their employees. This approach creates a sense of trust and respect among team members, elevating employee morale to new heights.

When employees feel that their leaders genuinely care about their welfare, they become more motivated to perform at their best. Ethical leaders create an inclusive environment where open communication and collaboration are encouraged. This fosters a sense of belonging and teamwork, which in turn boosts morale and motivation. Employees are more likely to go the extra mile and take ownership of their work when they feel valued and appreciated by their leaders.

Moreover, ethical leaders set clear expectations and hold their employees accountable for their actions. By establishing a strong ethical framework, leaders provide guidance and direction, ensuring that everyone understands the importance of ethical behavior in the workplace. This clarity enhances employee motivation, as individuals know that their efforts contribute to the overall success of the organization while upholding ethical standards.

In addition, ethical leaders promote a culture of continuous learning and growth. They invest in their employees' professional development, providing opportunities for training, mentorship, and advancement. This commitment to personal and professional growth inspires employees to develop their skills and knowledge, leading to increased job satisfaction and motivation.

Ultimately, the influence of ethical leadership on employee morale and motivation is undeniable. By creating a positive work environment, fostering trust, setting clear expectations, and investing in employee development, ethical leaders empower individuals to thrive in their personal and professional lives. When businesses prioritize ethical leadership, they not only benefit from improved employee morale and motivation but also contribute to a more ethical and sustainable business world as a whole.

"Ethics in Action: Empowering Every Individual in Business" is an invaluable resource for anyone interested in understanding the impact of ethical leadership on employee morale and motivation. This book provides practical insights, real-life examples, and actionable strategies to help individuals and organizations harness the power of ethical leadership and create a positive, productive, and ethical work environment. Whether you are a business owner, manager, or employee, this book will equip you with the knowledge and tools to make a difference in your workplace and contribute to a more ethical and empowering business world.

Empowering Individuals through Ethical Leadership Practices

In today's rapidly changing business landscape, ethical leadership practices have emerged as a crucial factor in empowering individuals and fostering a culture of integrity within organizations. Ethical leadership goes beyond mere compliance with laws and regulations; it involves a commitment to moral values, fairness, and accountability. This subchapter aims to explore the significance of ethical leadership practices and how they can empower every individual in business.

Ethical leadership is characterized by transparency, honesty, and a strong sense of responsibility. It provides a framework for decision-making that takes into account the welfare of all stakeholders, including employees, customers, shareholders, and the broader community. By adhering to ethical principles, leaders create an environment of trust, where individuals feel safe to voice their opinions, challenge the status quo, and contribute their unique perspectives.

One of the key aspects of ethical leadership is leading by example. When leaders demonstrate integrity and ethical behavior, it sets a powerful precedent for others to follow. By embracing ethical values, leaders inspire individuals to uphold the highest standards of conduct, fostering a culture of ethical awareness and responsibility throughout the organization.

Ethical leadership practices also promote personal growth and development. By encouraging open communication and active listening, leaders create opportunities for individuals to voice their concerns, share their ideas, and contribute to decision-making processes. This inclusive approach empowers individuals by recognizing their worth and providing them with a sense of ownership and autonomy.

Furthermore, ethical leadership practices foster a sense of purpose and meaning in the workplace. When individuals feel that their work aligns with their personal values and contributes to a larger societal good, they are more motivated, engaged, and fulfilled. Ethical leaders inspire individuals to become agents of positive change, encouraging them to go beyond their self-interests and contribute to the well-being of others.

In conclusion, ethical leadership practices play a pivotal role in empowering every individual in business. By promoting transparency, accountability, and fairness, ethical leaders create an environment of trust and integrity. They lead by example, inspire personal growth, and foster a sense of purpose. In doing so, they empower individuals to become ethical leaders themselves, driving positive change and creating a more ethical and sustainable business environment for all.

Chapter 3: Creating an Ethical Organizational Culture

Developing and Communicating Ethical Values and Standards

In the ever-evolving world of business, maintaining and upholding ethical values and standards is of utmost importance. Companies that prioritize ethical conduct not only benefit society as a whole but also foster an environment of trust, integrity, and long-term success. This subchapter aims to shed light on the significance of developing and effectively communicating ethical values and standards within the realm of business ethics.

Ethical values serve as guiding principles that shape the behavior and decision-making process of individuals and organizations. They define what is right and wrong, provide a moral compass, and establish a foundation for ethical conduct. Developing ethical values involves an introspective journey that requires businesses to evaluate their core beliefs, mission, and purpose. By identifying the values that align with their objectives, companies can create a framework that guides their actions and ensures ethical behavior becomes an integral part of their culture.

Once ethical values are established, effective communication becomes crucial. Businesses must articulate these values clearly and consistently to all stakeholders, including employees, customers, suppliers, and partners. Communication channels such as employee handbooks, codes of conduct, and training programs should be utilized to educate individuals about the ethical standards expected of them. Regular discussions, workshops, and seminars can further reinforce these values and encourage ethical decision-making in day-to-day operations.

Moreover, it is essential for businesses to lead by example. Leaders play a pivotal role in setting the tone for ethical behavior within an organization. By demonstrating integrity, transparency, and fairness in their actions, leaders inspire others to follow suit. Ethical conduct should be rewarded and recognized, creating a positive incentive for employees to uphold these values.

Developing and communicating ethical values and standards also involves addressing ethical dilemmas and conflicts. Businesses should establish mechanisms that allow individuals to report unethical behavior without fear of reprisal. Whistleblower protection policies, anonymous reporting channels, and open-door policies can encourage employees to come forward and help rectify any ethical breaches. By promptly addressing and resolving ethical concerns, businesses reinforce their commitment to ethical conduct and nurture a culture of trust and accountability.

In conclusion, developing and communicating ethical values and standards is paramount for businesses operating in the realm of business ethics. By aligning their actions with ethical principles, companies can gain a competitive edge, enhance their reputation, and contribute to the betterment of society. Through effective communication and leadership, businesses can empower every individual to make ethical choices, fostering a culture of integrity and responsibility that transcends the business world.

Implementing Ethical Codes of Conduct

In today's rapidly evolving business landscape, ethical behavior has become more important than ever before. It is no longer enough for companies to simply have a set of values or a mission statement; they must actively implement ethical codes of conduct to guide their actions and decision-making processes. This subchapter explores the significance of ethical codes of conduct in business and provides practical insights on how organizations can effectively implement them.

Ethical codes of conduct serve as a roadmap for individuals within an organization, outlining expected behaviors, promoting transparency, and fostering a culture of integrity. By providing clear guidelines, these codes help employees make ethical decisions when faced with complex dilemmas. They also establish a framework for accountability and ensure that all stakeholders are treated fairly and with respect.

Implementing ethical codes of conduct begins with top-level commitment and leadership. It is crucial for organizational leaders to demonstrate their dedication to ethical principles and act as role models for their teams. This involves integrating ethical considerations into the company's mission and vision, and communicating these values consistently throughout the organization.

To effectively implement ethical codes of conduct, organizations should establish a robust system for training and education. This ensures that employees are aware of the ethical guidelines and understand their implications. Regular training sessions can be conducted to reinforce ethical behavior and encourage employees to voice their concerns or seek guidance when faced with ethical dilemmas. Additionally, organizations can facilitate discussions and workshops to promote ethical decision-making skills among employees.

Another key aspect of implementing ethical codes of conduct is establishing mechanisms for monitoring and enforcement. Regular audits can be conducted to assess compliance with the codes and identify areas for improvement. Whistleblower hotlines or anonymous reporting channels can be set up to encourage employees to report any unethical practices without fear of retaliation. It is also essential to have a disciplinary process in place to address violations of the codes and take appropriate actions.

Ultimately, implementing ethical codes of conduct is a continuous process that requires ongoing review and refinement. As businesses evolve, ethical considerations may change, and codes need to be regularly updated to reflect these changes. By actively promoting ethical behavior and integrating it into every aspect of the organization, businesses can create a culture of trust, integrity, and sustainability.

In conclusion, ethical codes of conduct are essential for businesses to navigate the complex ethical landscape. They provide a framework for decision-making, promote accountability, and foster a culture of integrity. By implementing ethical codes of conduct, organizations empower individuals to make ethical choices, creating a positive impact on their stakeholders and the broader society.

Fostering Ethical Decision-Making through Organizational Policies and Procedures

In today's dynamic business environment, ethical decision-making is of paramount importance. It not only helps businesses maintain their reputation but also plays a vital role in building trust among stakeholders, including employees, customers, and investors. To empower every individual in business to make ethical decisions, organizations must establish robust policies and procedures that guide their behavior and actions.

Organizational policies and procedures serve as a framework for ethical decision-making by providing employees with clear guidelines and expectations. These guidelines ensure that individuals understand what is considered ethical behavior within the organization and what actions are deemed unacceptable. By setting these standards, organizations create a culture where ethical decision-making is both encouraged and expected.

One of the key aspects of fostering ethical decision-making is establishing a code of conduct. This code outlines the organization's values and principles and serves as a reference point for employees in their daily decision-making processes. It helps employees understand the ethical implications of their actions and provides guidance on how to navigate ethical dilemmas.

Additionally, organizations should implement training programs that educate employees on ethical decision-making. These programs can include case studies, role-playing exercises, and discussions that challenge individuals to consider various ethical scenarios. By providing employees with the necessary tools and knowledge, organizations empower them to make informed decisions that align with ethical principles.

Furthermore, organizations must create channels for reporting ethical concerns or violations without fear of retaliation. This can be done through anonymous reporting mechanisms or designated individuals within the organization who are responsible for addressing ethical issues. By encouraging whistleblowing and ensuring the confidentiality of those reporting, organizations create an environment where ethical concerns can be raised and addressed promptly.

To reinforce ethical decision-making, organizations should also establish a system of rewards and recognition that acknowledges individuals who consistently demonstrate ethical behavior. This can include public recognition, bonuses, or career advancement opportunities. By incentivizing ethical behavior, organizations create a culture where individuals are motivated to act in an ethical manner.

In conclusion, fostering ethical decision-making through organizational policies and procedures is crucial for businesses in today's competitive landscape. By establishing clear guidelines, providing training, and creating reporting mechanisms, organizations empower every individual to make ethical choices. Ultimately, this not only benefits the organization but also contributes to a more ethical and responsible business environment as a whole.

Chapter 4: Ethical Decision-Making Models and Approaches

The Utilitarian Approach

In the realm of business ethics, various theories and frameworks have been developed to guide decision-making processes and ensure ethical conduct. One such theory is the utilitarian approach, which emphasizes the importance of maximizing overall happiness or utility for the greatest number of people. This subchapter explores the utilitarian approach and its application in the context of business ethics.

The utilitarian approach is rooted in the concept of consequentialism, which asserts that the morality of an action is determined by its consequences. According to this approach, an action is considered ethically right if it produces the greatest amount of good for the greatest number of individuals. In business ethics, this means that decisions should be made with the objective of maximizing overall well-being and minimizing harm to stakeholders.

One key aspect of the utilitarian approach is the consideration of all parties affected by a decision. This includes not only shareholders and employees but also customers, suppliers, the local community, and even the environment. By taking into account the interests and well-being of all stakeholders, businesses can ensure a fair and ethical decision-making process.

However, the utilitarian approach is not without its challenges. Critics argue that it may neglect the rights of individuals or minority groups, as the focus is on the overall happiness of the majority. Additionally, quantifying and measuring happiness or utility can be complex, making it difficult to objectively assess the consequences of a decision.

Nevertheless, the utilitarian approach offers valuable insights for businesses seeking to be ethical and responsible. By considering the potential consequences of their actions and striving to maximize overall happiness, businesses can create a positive impact on society. This approach can inform decisions related to product development, marketing strategies, supply chain management, and even corporate social responsibility initiatives.

In conclusion, the utilitarian approach provides a framework for ethical decision-making in the realm of business. By prioritizing the overall happiness and well-being of stakeholders, businesses can strive to create a positive impact on society. However, it is important to recognize the limitations and challenges associated with this approach, and to constantly evaluate and adapt ethical frameworks to the ever-evolving business landscape. Ultimately, the utilitarian approach empowers individuals in business to make choices that not only benefit their organizations but also create a more ethical and sustainable world for all.

The Deontological Approach

In the realm of Business Ethics, the Deontological Approach is a significant ethical framework that holds immense relevance. It is a moral philosophy that focuses on duty, obligation, and adherence to a set of rules or principles. This approach emphasizes the inherent rightness or wrongness of an action, regardless of its consequences. In other words, it asserts that actions are intrinsically good or bad based on whether they align with certain ethical principles or duties.

At its core, the Deontological Approach emphasizes the importance of following moral rules and duties, regardless of the outcomes they may produce. It looks beyond the consequences and instead focuses on the intentions and motivations behind an action. For instance, a deontologist would argue that telling the truth is inherently good, regardless of the negative consequences it may bring.

The Deontological Approach can be traced back to the works of renowned philosophers like Immanuel Kant and his concept of categorical imperatives. According to Kant, there are certain moral duties that are universally binding on all individuals, regardless of their circumstances. These duties are derived from reason and rationality rather than personal preferences or desires.

In a business context, the Deontological Approach can guide decision-making processes and help individuals in organizations navigate complex ethical dilemmas. By adhering to a set of ethical principles and duties, individuals can ensure that their actions align with their moral obligations. For instance, a deontologist might argue that protecting the privacy of customers is an essential duty, regardless of the potential financial benefits that may arise from breaching that privacy.

However, the Deontological Approach is not without its criticisms. One major critique is that it can be too rigid and inflexible, failing to account for the complexities of real-world situations. Critics argue that a strict adherence to rules and duties may lead to moral absolutism and overlook the nuances and context of a particular situation.

In conclusion, the Deontological Approach is a crucial framework within Business Ethics. It emphasizes the significance of moral duties and adherence to ethical principles, irrespective of the consequences. By considering this approach, individuals in business can make decisions that are guided by their moral obligations, ultimately contributing to a more ethical and responsible business environment.

The Virtue Ethics Approach

In the realm of business ethics, there are various ethical frameworks that guide individuals and organizations on how to make morally sound decisions. One such approach is Virtue Ethics, which focuses on the development of good character traits and virtues in individuals.

Virtue Ethics places emphasis on the idea that ethical behavior stems from the cultivation of virtuous traits. It suggests that every individual, regardless of their role in the business world, should strive to develop and embody virtues such as honesty, integrity, compassion, and fairness. By doing so, individuals can make ethical decisions that benefit not only themselves but also their colleagues, customers, and the society at large.

This approach encourages individuals to reflect on their values and personal qualities, aiming to become better versions of themselves. By consciously developing virtues, individuals can enhance their moral character and become more ethical in their business practices. For instance, a business leader who values honesty and integrity will be more likely to make decisions that are transparent and fair, even in challenging situations.

In the context of business ethics, the Virtue Ethics approach acknowledges that ethical decision-making is not always straightforward. It recognizes that ethical dilemmas can be complex and require careful consideration of various factors. However, by grounding decisions in virtues, individuals can navigate these challenges with a moral compass that guides them towards the most ethically sound course of action.

Furthermore, the Virtue Ethics approach recognizes the importance of fostering a virtuous organizational culture. It highlights the significance of creating an environment that promotes and rewards virtues such as trust, respect, and empathy. By embedding these virtues into the fabric of the organization, businesses can foster a sense of ethical responsibility among its employees and contribute positively to the broader society.

In conclusion, the Virtue Ethics approach in business ethics encourages individuals to cultivate virtuous traits and values. It recognizes the importance of personal character development, ethical decision-making, and the creation of a virtuous organizational culture. By adopting this approach, individuals can empower themselves to make ethical choices that benefit not only their business but also society as a whole.

Integrating Multiple Approaches for Ethical Decision-Making

Ethical decision-making is a critical aspect of conducting business in today's complex and interconnected world. As the global marketplace becomes more diverse and interconnected, it is essential for individuals in business to navigate ethical dilemmas with confidence and integrity. To achieve this, integrating multiple approaches to ethical decision-making can be highly effective, providing a comprehensive framework that enables individuals to make informed choices aligned with their values and the expectations of society.

One approach to ethical decision-making is the deontological perspective, which focuses on following rules and principles. This approach emphasizes the importance of duty and moral obligations, ensuring that individuals act in a manner consistent with ethical standards. By considering the inherent rights and wrongs of a situation, individuals can make decisions that prioritize ethical considerations, even when faced with conflicting interests or pressures.

Another approach is consequentialism, which evaluates the outcomes of actions to determine their ethical value. This approach encourages individuals to consider the consequences of their decisions, taking into account the potential impact on stakeholders, society, and the environment. By weighing the benefits and harms associated with various courses of action, individuals can make choices that maximize overall well-being and minimize potential harm.

Furthermore, the virtue ethics approach focuses on cultivating moral character and personal virtues. This approach emphasizes the importance of developing virtues such as honesty, compassion, and fairness, which guide individuals' behavior and decision-making. By embodying these virtues, individuals can make ethical decisions that align with their core values and contribute to the development of a more ethical business environment.

Integrating these approaches allows individuals to consider multiple perspectives when faced with ethical dilemmas. By combining the deontological, consequentialist, and virtue ethics frameworks, individuals can gain a more holistic understanding of ethical decision-making, enabling them to make well-informed choices that balance multiple considerations.

In addition to integrating multiple ethical approaches, it is crucial for individuals in business to engage in ongoing self-reflection and ethical awareness. This involves continuously evaluating and refining personal values, beliefs, and ethical principles. By regularly examining one's own ethical compass, individuals can ensure that their decision-making aligns with their evolving understanding of ethics and the demands of the business environment.

Ultimately, integrating multiple approaches for ethical decision-making empowers individuals to navigate the complex landscape of business ethics with confidence and integrity. By considering deontological principles, evaluating consequences, and cultivating virtues, individuals can make decisions that not only benefit their organizations but also contribute to a more ethical and sustainable business world.

Chapter 5: Identifying Ethical Dilemmas in Business

Recognizing Ethical Issues and Challenges

In today's fast-paced and interconnected business world, ethics play a crucial role in shaping the way organizations operate and individuals conduct themselves. Recognizing ethical issues and challenges is an essential skill for every individual involved in the business industry. Whether you are a seasoned entrepreneur, a manager, or an employee, understanding and addressing ethical dilemmas can help navigate the complex landscape of business ethics.

This subchapter aims to empower every individual by providing insights and strategies to identify and tackle ethical issues effectively. By exploring various scenarios and case studies, readers will gain a deeper understanding of the ethical challenges that arise in different business contexts.

One of the key aspects of recognizing ethical issues is being able to distinguish between right and wrong, and understanding the consequences of our actions. Sometimes, ethical dilemmas may arise when there is a conflict between personal values and organizational goals. It is essential to develop a moral compass that guides decision-making in such situations, considering the long-term impact on stakeholders and the overall reputation of the organization.

Additionally, recognizing ethical issues requires an understanding of the external factors that can influence decision-making. This subchapter will shed light on the role of social, cultural, and legal frameworks in shaping ethical standards in business. It will also explore the impact of globalization and technological advancements on ethical considerations, as businesses operate in an increasingly interconnected and diverse world.

Furthermore, this subchapter will delve into the challenges that arise from ethical dilemmas in today's rapidly changing business landscape. It will discuss issues such as corporate social responsibility, sustainability, and the ethical implications of emerging technologies. By examining real-world examples and engaging in critical thinking exercises, readers will develop a proactive mindset to anticipate and address ethical challenges before they become crises.

Ultimately, recognizing ethical issues and challenges is not only about avoiding legal trouble or reputational damage but also about fostering a culture of trust, integrity, and fairness within organizations. This subchapter aims to empower every individual, regardless of their role or background, to become ethical leaders in their respective fields. By equipping readers with the necessary tools and knowledge, we can collectively create a business environment that upholds ethical principles and promotes the well-being of all stakeholders involved.

Understanding the Factors that Contribute to Ethical Dilemmas

Ethics in Action: Empowering Every Individual in Business

Ethical dilemmas are a common occurrence in the business world, affecting individuals at all levels of an organization. To effectively navigate these moral challenges, it is crucial to understand the factors that contribute to their formation. This subchapter aims to shed light on the various elements that give rise to ethical dilemmas, allowing every individual in business to be better equipped to make ethical decisions.

One significant factor is the pressure to achieve organizational goals and targets. In today's competitive landscape, businesses are often driven by profit margins and market share. This relentless pursuit of success can create an environment where individuals may feel compelled to compromise their ethical standards to meet these objectives. The pressure to perform can lead to decisions that disregard ethical considerations, creating ethical dilemmas for those involved.

Another factor is the influence of organizational culture and leadership. The values and ethos set by leaders trickle down to shape the behavior of employees. If an organization does not prioritize ethical conduct or lacks a strong ethical framework, it can foster an environment where unethical practices are more likely to occur. In such cases, employees may find themselves torn between adhering to their personal moral compass and conforming to the prevailing organizational culture.

Individual factors also contribute to ethical dilemmas. People have their own unique set of values, beliefs, and principles that guide their decision-making process. However, these personal values can sometimes clash with the values espoused by the organization, leading to ethical conflicts. Additionally, factors such as personal ambition, financial incentives, and peer pressure can exert influence over an individual's ethical choices, further complicating the decision-making process.

External factors, such as industry norms and societal expectations, also play a role in ethical dilemmas. Industries where unethical practices are prevalent may create an environment where individuals are more likely to face ethical conflicts. Similarly, societal values and expectations can shape the ethical landscape within a business, with actions that were once considered acceptable becoming ethically questionable due to shifting societal norms.

Understanding these factors is essential for every individual in business, as it enables them to identify potential ethical dilemmas and make more informed decisions. By recognizing the pressures, influences, and conflicts that contribute to ethical dilemmas, individuals can proactively seek solutions that align with their personal values and ethical standards. Furthermore, this awareness empowers individuals to drive positive change within their organizations by advocating for ethical practices and promoting a culture of integrity.

In conclusion, ethical dilemmas are a complex issue faced by individuals in all areas of business. Recognizing the factors that contribute to their formation is essential in navigating these challenges. By understanding the pressures of achieving organizational goals, the impact of organizational culture and leadership, individual factors, and external influences, individuals can make more ethical decisions and contribute to the development of a more ethically conscious business environment.

Ethical Decision-Making in Complex Situations

In today's fast-paced and interconnected business world, individuals often find themselves facing complex ethical dilemmas. These situations can arise due to various factors such as conflicting values, competing interests, or ambiguous circumstances. Ethical decision-making in such complex situations requires a thoughtful and principled approach to ensure that individuals uphold moral standards while navigating the intricacies of the business environment.

One crucial aspect of ethical decision-making is the recognition that there is rarely a clear-cut answer to complex ethical dilemmas. These situations often involve multiple stakeholders with diverse perspectives and interests. Therefore, it becomes essential to consider various ethical frameworks and principles to guide decision-making.

One widely used ethical framework is consequentialism, which focuses on the outcomes or consequences of an action. In complex situations, individuals must carefully evaluate the potential consequences of their actions on all stakeholders involved. This approach requires considering both short-term and long-term impacts, as well as the potential risks and benefits associated with each decision.

Another ethical framework that individuals can employ is deontology, which emphasizes the adherence to moral duties and principles. In complex situations, individuals must identify and prioritize the ethical principles that should guide their actions. This may involve weighing conflicting principles and determining which principle holds more weight in a particular context.

Additionally, ethical decision-making in complex situations often requires individuals to engage in critical thinking and ethical considering the potential trade-offs and impacts on various stakeholders, businesses can make more informed and ethical decisions.

Additionally, businesses should be aware of the potential biases that can influence decision-making. Confirmation bias, for instance, can lead to the favoring of certain stakeholders' perspectives over others. To mitigate this, it is essential to gather diverse opinions and perspectives and critically evaluate all available information before making decisions.

In conclusion, considering stakeholder perspectives is a fundamental aspect of business ethics. By recognizing the power dynamics, promoting inclusivity, and understanding the interconnectedness of stakeholders, businesses can make more ethical and responsible decisions. This not only helps to build trust and stronger relationships but also contributes to the overall well-being of society. It is crucial for every individual involved in business to embrace this perspective and strive to empower all stakeholders through ethical decision-making.

Seeking Guidance from Ethical Experts or Professionals

In the complex world of business ethics, seeking guidance from ethical experts or professionals can be invaluable for individuals navigating ethical dilemmas in their professional lives. These experts possess a deep understanding of ethical principles, frameworks, and industry best practices, and can offer valuable insights and perspectives that can help individuals make informed decisions aligned with ethical standards.

Ethical experts or professionals come from various backgrounds, including academia, consulting firms, and industry-specific organizations. They have devoted their careers to studying, researching, and promoting ethical behavior in business. Their expertise covers a wide range of ethical issues, such as conflicts of interest, corporate social responsibility, fair trade, and environmental sustainability, among others.

When faced with an ethical dilemma, seeking guidance from these experts can provide individuals with a fresh perspective on the situation. They can help analyze the ethical dimensions, potential consequences, and alternative courses of action. By engaging in thoughtful discussions with these professionals, individuals can explore different viewpoints, challenge their own biases, and gain a more comprehensive understanding of the ethical implications of their choices.

Ethical experts or professionals also play a crucial role in providing guidance and support in the development and implementation of ethical policies and practices within organizations. They can assist in crafting a strong ethical framework that aligns with the values and goals of the organization. They can also help design training programs to educate employees about ethical principles and equip them with the necessary tools to handle ethical challenges effectively.

In addition to seeking guidance from ethical experts or professionals, individuals can also benefit from engaging in ethical communities and networks. These communities provide a platform for like-minded individuals to share experiences, discuss ethical dilemmas, and learn from one another. They offer a supportive environment where individuals can seek guidance, advice, and encouragement from peers who understand the challenges of navigating business ethics.

In conclusion, seeking guidance from ethical experts or professionals is crucial for individuals in the realm of business ethics. Their knowledge, experience, and insights can empower individuals to make informed decisions, navigate ethical dilemmas, and contribute to a more ethical business environment. By engaging with these experts and participating in ethical communities, individuals can strengthen their ethical compass and become ethical leaders in their respective fields.

Ethical Decision-Making in Group Settings

In today's complex business world, where collaboration and teamwork are essential for success, ethical decision-making in group settings holds significant importance. As businesses strive to maintain their competitive edge, it becomes crucial for every individual to understand the ethical implications of their decisions and actions within a group dynamic. This subchapter, titled "Ethical Decision-Making in Group Settings," aims to empower every individual in business by providing insights into the challenges and strategies involved in maintaining ethical conduct within group settings.

The dynamics of group decision-making can often lead to ethical dilemmas, as conflicting interests, power dynamics, and individual biases come into play. However, by fostering a culture of ethical awareness and accountability, individuals can navigate these challenges and make well-informed decisions that align with their personal values and the broader ethical standards of the organization.

The first step towards ethical decision-making in group settings is establishing clear communication channels and fostering an environment that encourages open dialogue. By promoting a culture of transparency and actively seeking diverse perspectives, individuals can gain a comprehensive understanding of the ethical implications of their decisions and ensure everyone's voices are heard.

Additionally, it is crucial to establish a framework for ethical decision-making within the group. This framework should include guidelines for identifying and evaluating ethical issues, considering the potential consequences of actions, and determining the best course of action that aligns with ethical principles. By having a structured approach, individuals can navigate complex ethical dilemmas in a systematic and thoughtful manner.

Furthermore, ethical decision-making in group settings requires individuals to be aware of their own biases and prejudices. By actively reflecting on personal values and biases, individuals can mitigate the impact of these factors on decision-making processes. Additionally, embracing diversity within the group can help challenge preconceived notions and enhance the quality of ethical decision-making.

Lastly, accountability is crucial in ensuring ethical decision-making in group settings. Each individual must take responsibility for their actions and be willing to address any ethical concerns that arise. By holding oneself accountable and encouraging others to do the same, individuals can maintain integrity within the group and foster a culture of ethical conduct.

In conclusion, ethical decision-making in group settings is a critical aspect of business ethics that empowers every individual to make responsible and morally sound choices. By fostering open communication, establishing a decision-making framework, addressing personal biases, and promoting accountability, individuals can navigate ethical dilemmas within groups and contribute to a more ethical business environment.

Chapter 7: Ethical Communication and Transparency in Business

The Role of Open and Honest Communication in Ethical Decision-Making

In today's complex and interconnected business world, ethical decision-making has become more important than ever. The choices we make as individuals and organizations can have far-reaching consequences, impacting not only our own reputation and success, but also the well-being of our employees, customers, and society as a whole. One of the key elements that underpins ethical decision-making is open and honest communication.

Open and honest communication can be seen as the foundation of ethical behavior in business. It involves sharing information transparently, engaging in meaningful dialogue, and actively listening to others. When individuals and organizations prioritize open and honest communication, they create an environment where ethical decision-making can thrive.

First and foremost, open and honest communication helps to build trust. Trust is the cornerstone of any successful business relationship, and without it, ethical decision-making becomes nearly impossible. When employees, customers, and stakeholders feel that they can rely on open and honest communication, they are more likely to trust the intentions and actions of the individuals and organizations involved. This trust forms the basis for ethical decision-making, as it allows for the free exchange of ideas, concerns, and feedback.

Furthermore, open and honest communication fosters a culture of accountability. When individuals feel comfortable speaking up and expressing their views, they are more likely to take responsibility for their actions and decisions. This culture of accountability is crucial for ethical decision-making, as it ensures that individuals are aware of the potential consequences of their choices and are willing to take ownership of them.

Open and honest communication also promotes ethical decision-making through the inclusion of diverse perspectives. By encouraging individuals to share their viewpoints and actively listening to them, organizations can gain a deeper understanding of the ethical implications of their choices. This diversity of perspectives helps to identify potential ethical dilemmas and enables organizations to make more informed decisions that consider a wide range of ethical considerations.

In conclusion, open and honest communication plays a vital role in ethical decision-making in the realm of business ethics. By building trust, fostering accountability, and including diverse perspectives, it creates an environment where individuals and organizations can make ethical choices that benefit not only themselves but also their stakeholders and society as a whole. Emphasizing open and honest communication is a fundamental step towards empowering every individual in business to act ethically and make a positive impact on the world.

Building Trust and Credibility through Transparent Practices

In today's business world, trust and credibility are vital for success. Customers, employees, and stakeholders all seek to engage with businesses that demonstrate ethical behavior and transparent practices. Building trust and credibility should be a top priority for every organization, regardless of its size or industry. This subchapter explores the importance of transparency in building trust and credibility, and how it can empower every individual in business.

Transparency in business refers to the practice of openly sharing information, decisions, and processes with stakeholders. It involves being honest, accountable, and providing clear communication. When businesses adopt transparent practices, they create an environment that fosters trust and credibility.

Customers are increasingly concerned about the ethical practices of the businesses they engage with. They want to know that the products they purchase are ethically sourced and produced. By being transparent about sourcing methods, supply chain processes, and environmental impact, businesses can build trust with their customers. This trust leads to customer loyalty and positive brand reputation.

Transparency is also crucial in building trust with employees. When employees feel that their organization is open and honest, they are more likely to be engaged, motivated, and loyal. Transparent practices help employees understand the decision-making processes, which creates a sense of fairness and trust. This, in turn, leads to a more productive and harmonious work environment.

Furthermore, stakeholders, including investors and partners, are more likely to engage with businesses that operate transparently. Financial transparency, such as disclosing accurate financial statements and being upfront about risks, builds credibility and attracts potential investors.

Implementing transparent practices requires a commitment to ethical behavior and a willingness to share information. Organizations should establish clear policies and guidelines for transparency, ensuring that they align with ethical standards. Communication channels should be established to facilitate open dialogue and provide opportunities for feedback from stakeholders. Regular reporting and audits should be conducted to ensure transparency is maintained throughout the organization.

In conclusion, building trust and credibility through transparent practices is essential for every individual in business. It creates a positive environment that attracts customers, engages employees, and builds credibility with stakeholders. By adopting transparent practices, organizations can empower every individual to act ethically and contribute to a more sustainable and trustworthy business ecosystem.

Addressing Ethical Concerns and Whistleblowing

In today's business landscape, ethical concerns have become more prevalent than ever before. Companies are expected to operate with integrity and transparency, but unfortunately, not all organizations meet these expectations. This subchapter delves into the importance of addressing ethical concerns and the role of whistleblowing in promoting a culture of ethics in business.

Ethics in business is not just a moral obligation; it is also a strategic imperative. Organizations that prioritize ethics are more likely to gain the trust and loyalty of customers, employees, and stakeholders. Moreover, ethical practices foster a positive work environment and create a competitive advantage. By addressing ethical concerns head-on, businesses can avoid reputational damage, legal repercussions, and financial losses.

The first step in addressing ethical concerns is to establish a strong ethical framework within the organization. This framework should include a code of conduct that clearly outlines expected behaviors, as well as mechanisms to report ethical violations. Employees should feel empowered to speak up when they witness unethical practices, without fear of retaliation.

Whistleblowing plays a crucial role in addressing ethical concerns. Whistleblowers are individuals who expose wrongdoing within an organization. They act as ethical gatekeepers, safeguarding the interests of stakeholders and society at large. Whistleblowers have played a significant role in uncovering corporate scandals and bringing unethical practices to light.

Unfortunately, whistleblowing can be a daunting task for individuals. Fear of retaliation, ostracization, and job loss often deter employees from reporting ethical violations. To overcome these barriers, organizations must create a safe and supportive environment for whistleblowers. This can be achieved by implementing anonymous reporting mechanisms, providing legal protections, and offering emotional support to those who come forward.

In addition to organizational support, society as a whole must encourage and protect whistleblowers. Legal frameworks should be in place to safeguard their rights and provide incentives for reporting unethical behavior. By doing so, we can foster a culture where whistleblowing is seen as a responsible act, rather than a betrayal.

Addressing ethical concerns and promoting whistleblowing is not just the responsibility of organizations; it is a collective effort. Each one of us has a role to play in upholding ethical standards in business. Whether as employees, customers, or stakeholders, we must demand accountability and transparency from the organizations we engage with. By empowering every individual to act ethically, we can create a business environment that thrives on integrity and promotes the common good.

In conclusion, addressing ethical concerns and promoting whistleblowing is vital for the success and sustainability of businesses. By establishing a strong ethical framework, supporting whistleblowers, and fostering a culture of accountability, organizations can ensure that ethical concerns are addressed promptly and effectively. Let us all join hands in empowering every individual to act ethically, thus shaping a future where business ethics are the norm rather than the exception.

Chapter 8: Ethical Leadership and the Bottom Line

The Relationship between Ethical Leadership and Organizational Performance

In today's dynamic and competitive business landscape, the role of ethical leadership in driving organizational performance has become increasingly evident. Ethics in Action: Empowering Every Individual in Business delves into the crucial link between ethical leadership and organizational success, shedding light on how ethical behavior at the top can impact the entire company.

Ethical leadership is not just a buzzword; it is a fundamental aspect of effective management that has a profound influence on an organization's performance. It involves leaders who demonstrate integrity, fairness, and transparency in their decision-making and interactions with employees, stakeholders, and the broader community. By embodying these ethical values, leaders set the tone for the entire organization and create an ethical culture that permeates every aspect of the business.

Why does ethical leadership matter to every individual in business? The answer lies in the positive impact it has on organizational performance. Research has consistently shown that companies with ethical leaders tend to outperform their competitors in multiple areas. Employees are more engaged, committed, and motivated when they trust their leaders and believe in the organization's ethical values. This, in turn, leads to higher productivity, improved teamwork, and enhanced innovation.

Moreover, ethical leadership fosters a positive reputation for the organization, enhancing its brand image and attracting top talent and loyal customers. When leaders prioritize ethics and social responsibility, they align the organization's goals with the needs and expectations of various stakeholders, including customers, employees, suppliers, and the community. This alignment builds trust and credibility, which translates into long-term success and sustainability.

However, the relationship between ethical leadership and organizational performance is not solely about financial gains. Ethical leaders also prioritize the well-being and development of their employees, creating a supportive and inclusive work environment. This, in turn, leads to higher job satisfaction, reduced turnover, and increased employee loyalty. By championing ethical behavior, leaders cultivate a sense of purpose and meaning within the organization, allowing individuals to connect their work with a greater societal impact.

In conclusion, the relationship between ethical leadership and organizational performance is a critical aspect of business ethics. Ethical leaders shape the ethical culture of an organization, fostering trust, engagement, and commitment among employees. This, in turn, leads to improved productivity, innovation, and a positive reputation, ultimately driving long-term success. Every individual in business has a role to play in promoting ethical leadership, as it empowers employees, enhances the organization's performance, and contributes to a more ethical and sustainable business environment.

The Long-Term Benefits of Ethical Decision-Making

Ethics in Action: Empowering Every Individual in Business

In an increasingly complex and interconnected world, ethical decision-making has emerged as a crucial aspect of successful business practices. Whether you are a business owner, an employee, or even a consumer, understanding the long-term benefits of ethical decision-making can have a profound impact on your professional and personal life.

One of the most significant advantages of ethical decision-making in business is the establishment of trust and credibility. When individuals consistently make ethical choices, they earn the respect and admiration of their colleagues, clients, and customers. This trust forms the foundation of strong professional relationships, leading to increased collaboration, loyalty, and ultimately, success.

Moreover, ethical decision-making fosters a positive work environment. By prioritizing moral values, businesses can create a culture of integrity and fairness. This, in turn, promotes employee satisfaction and engagement, resulting in enhanced productivity and innovation. When employees feel valued and supported, they are more likely to go the extra mile and contribute to the growth of the organization.

Ethical decision-making also helps organizations build a solid reputation in the market. In today's era of social media and instant information sharing, businesses cannot afford to overlook their ethical responsibilities. Companies that consistently make ethical choices are seen as reliable, responsible, and socially conscious. This positive reputation not only attracts loyal customers but also attracts top talent, investors, and partners, leading to long-term sustainability and growth.

Furthermore, ethical decision-making contributes to the overall well-being of society. By considering the broader impact of their actions, businesses can actively contribute to social causes, environmental sustainability, and community development. This sense of corporate citizenship not only benefits society but also enhances the brand's image and strengthens customer loyalty.

Ultimately, ethical decision-making is not just about compliance with laws and regulations; it is about doing what is right, even when no one is watching. It is about aligning personal and organizational values to create a positive and sustainable impact on the world. By embracing ethical decision-making, individuals and businesses can unlock a multitude of long-term benefits that go beyond financial success.

In conclusion, the long-term benefits of ethical decision-making are undeniable. From fostering trust and credibility to creating a positive work environment, building a solid reputation, and contributing to society, ethical behavior is a key driver of success in the business world. So, let us strive to make ethical choices, empower every individual in business, and create a better future for ourselves and generations to come.

Overcoming Challenges and Resistance to Ethical Practices

In the realm of business ethics, it is essential to not only understand the principles of ethical behavior but also the challenges and resistance that individuals and organizations may face when implementing ethical practices. Overcoming these obstacles is crucial to foster a culture of integrity and responsibility in business.

One of the common challenges encountered when promoting ethical practices is the resistance from stakeholders who prioritize short-term gains over long-term sustainability. In such cases, it becomes essential to educate and raise awareness about the benefits of ethical behavior. By highlighting the positive impact on reputation, customer loyalty, and employee satisfaction, businesses can gradually shift the mindset towards an ethical approach.

Another challenge lies in the complexity of ethical decision-making. Ethical dilemmas can often arise in business situations, which require careful analysis and consideration of various factors. This can lead to confusion and resistance, as individuals may find it difficult to navigate through these complexities. To overcome this challenge, it is crucial to provide training and support to employees, equipping them with the necessary tools to make informed ethical decisions.

Resistance to ethical practices can also stem from cultural differences and varying ethical standards across different regions and industries. Overcoming this challenge requires embracing diversity and acknowledging the need for cultural sensitivity. By engaging in open dialogue and fostering a culture of inclusivity, businesses can bridge the gap and find common ground in ethical practices that align with global standards.

Furthermore, implementing ethical practices may require significant changes in existing systems and processes, which can be met with resistance from within the organization. Overcoming this challenge necessitates strong leadership and effective change management strategies. Leaders must communicate the importance of ethical behavior, provide a clear roadmap for implementation, and involve employees at every level in the decision-making process. By creating a sense of ownership and collective responsibility, businesses can overcome internal resistance and drive positive change.

In conclusion, overcoming challenges and resistance to ethical practices is a crucial aspect of promoting a culture of integrity in business. By addressing resistance from stakeholders, providing training and support, embracing diversity, and implementing effective change management strategies, businesses can empower every individual to make ethical choices. Only by collectively overcoming these challenges can we create a sustainable and ethical future for businesses and society as a whole.

Chapter 9: Implementing Ethical Decision-Making in Business

Developing an Ethical Decision-Making Framework

In today's complex and fast-paced business environment, ethical decision-making has become a crucial skill for individuals at all levels of an organization. The ability to navigate the ethical dilemmas and challenges that arise in business is essential for maintaining trust, reputation, and ultimately, long-term success.

This subchapter aims to empower every individual in business with the knowledge and tools necessary to develop an ethical decision-making framework. Whether you are a business owner, manager, employee, or even a student preparing for a career in business, this chapter will provide you with practical guidance on how to approach ethical dilemmas.

The first step in developing an ethical decision-making framework is understanding the importance of ethics in business. Ethics goes beyond mere compliance with laws and regulations; it involves making decisions that are morally right and just. By adhering to ethical principles, businesses can build a culture of integrity, trust, and accountability that fosters long-term success.

Next, we explore various ethical theories and frameworks that can serve as a foundation for decision-making. From consequentialism to deontology, virtue ethics, and beyond, each theory offers a unique perspective on how to approach ethical dilemmas. By understanding these theories, individuals can evaluate the potential consequences, duties, and virtues associated with their decisions, and make more informed choices.

Building upon this theoretical foundation, we delve into the practical steps of an ethical decision-making process. This includes identifying the ethical dilemma, gathering relevant information, considering alternative courses of action, evaluating the consequences, and selecting the most ethical option. We also address the importance of consulting with others, seeking diverse perspectives, and considering the potential impact of decisions on various stakeholders.

Furthermore, we discuss the role of organizational culture and leadership in promoting ethical decision-making. We explore how organizations can establish ethical frameworks, codes of conduct, and training programs that empower individuals to make ethical choices. We also emphasize the importance of leadership in setting the tone from the top and modeling ethical behavior.

Finally, we provide real-life case studies and examples that illustrate the challenges and complexities of ethical decision-making in different business contexts. By analyzing these cases, readers can gain a deeper understanding of how ethical principles can be applied in practice and develop their own ethical decision-making skills.

In conclusion, developing an ethical decision-making framework is essential for individuals in every business niche. This subchapter equips readers with the knowledge, tools, and practical guidance needed to navigate ethical dilemmas, make informed choices, and contribute to a more ethical and responsible business environment. By empowering every individual in business with ethical decision-making skills, we can collectively drive positive change and shape a more sustainable future.

Training and Educating Employees on Ethical Practices

In today's fast-paced and ever-evolving business landscape, maintaining ethical practices is of paramount importance. Businesses are not just expected to generate profits, but also to conduct their operations with integrity, honesty, and social responsibility. To achieve this, organizations must invest in training and educating their employees on ethical practices.

Ethics in Action: Empowering Every Individual in Business is a comprehensive guide that emphasizes the significance of ethical behavior in the corporate world. This subchapter focuses on the vital role of training and educating employees in promoting and upholding ethical practices.

Training programs are essential to familiarize employees with the organization's code of conduct, policies, and industry regulations. By providing clear guidelines on ethical behavior, employees gain a better understanding of their roles and responsibilities in maintaining a positive work environment. These programs also emphasize the consequences of unethical practices, both for the individual and the organization as a whole.

Educating employees on ethical practices goes beyond simply outlining rules and regulations. It involves fostering a culture of ethics within the organization. This can be achieved through seminars, workshops, and interactive sessions that encourage open discussions on ethical dilemmas and real-life scenarios. By engaging employees in these discussions, they develop critical thinking skills and learn how to navigate complex ethical situations.

Moreover, organizations should consider incorporating case studies and role-playing exercises during training sessions. This allows employees to apply ethical principles to real-world scenarios, enabling them to make informed decisions when faced with ethical challenges. By actively involving employees in the learning process, organizations can foster a sense of ownership and commitment towards ethical practices.

It is crucial to remember that training and educating employees on ethical practices should be an ongoing process. As business ethics evolve, organizations must regularly update their training programs to address emerging ethical concerns. This ensures that employees stay informed about the latest ethical standards and are equipped to handle complex ethical dilemmas.

By investing in training and educating employees on ethical practices, businesses not only protect themselves from reputational damage and legal consequences but also build a culture of trust, transparency, and integrity. Ultimately, this fosters a positive work environment where employees feel empowered to make ethically sound decisions in all aspects of their professional lives.

Ethics in Action: Empowering Every Individual in Business is a valuable resource for individuals in all niches of business ethics. Whether you are an employee, manager, or business owner, this book provides practical insights and guidance on how to navigate ethical challenges and promote ethical practices within your organization. By prioritizing ethical training and education, we can create a business landscape that thrives on integrity and positively impacts society as a whole.

Evaluating and Monitoring Ethical Performance

In the world of business, ethical performance is a critical aspect that cannot be overlooked. It is not enough to simply have ethics policies in place; organizations must also evaluate and monitor their ethical performance to ensure that they are operating in an ethical and responsible manner. This subchapter will explore the importance of evaluating and monitoring ethical performance and provide practical guidance on how individuals and organizations can achieve this.

Evaluating ethical performance involves assessing the extent to which an organization adheres to its ethical standards and values. It requires a systematic review of processes, practices, and behaviors to identify areas where improvements can be made. By regularly evaluating ethical performance, organizations can identify potential ethical dilemmas and take proactive measures to mitigate any risks.

Monitoring ethical performance goes hand in hand with evaluation, as it involves ongoing surveillance to ensure that ethical standards are consistently being upheld. This can be achieved through various mechanisms, such as internal audits, employee surveys, and feedback channels. By continuously monitoring ethical performance, organizations can identify any deviations from their ethical standards and take prompt corrective actions.

One effective way to evaluate and monitor ethical performance is through the establishment of key performance indicators (KPIs) specifically tailored to measure ethical conduct. These KPIs can include metrics such as the number of ethical violations reported, the effectiveness of ethics training programs, and the level of employee satisfaction with the organization's ethical culture. By setting measurable KPIs, organizations can track their progress and identify areas that require improvement.

Another crucial aspect of evaluating and monitoring ethical performance is fostering a culture of transparency and accountability. This involves creating an environment where employees feel comfortable reporting ethical concerns and where there are clear consequences for unethical behavior. Organizations can achieve this by establishing anonymous reporting mechanisms, conducting regular ethics training programs, and implementing a robust disciplinary process.

In conclusion, evaluating and monitoring ethical performance is a vital component of effective business ethics. It ensures that organizations are consistently adhering to their ethical standards and values, and helps them identify areas for improvement. By establishing KPIs, fostering a culture of transparency, and implementing monitoring mechanisms, individuals and organizations can empower themselves to uphold the highest ethical standards in their business practices.

Chapter 10: Conclusion: Empowering Every Individual in Business

Recap of Key Concepts and Insights

In this subchapter, we will take a moment to recap the key concepts and insights discussed so far in "Ethics in Action: Empowering Every Individual in Business." Our aim is to provide a comprehensive overview of the fundamental ideas and principles that can guide individuals in navigating the complex world of business ethics.

At its core, this book seeks to empower every individual, regardless of their position or role in the business world, to make ethical decisions and contribute to a more responsible and sustainable business environment. We firmly believe that ethics should not be confined to a select few, but rather should be embraced by everyone in order to foster a culture of integrity and accountability.

Throughout the book, we have explored various ethical frameworks, such as consequentialism, deontology, and virtue ethics, to help readers develop a solid foundation for ethical decision-making. We have highlighted the importance of considering the consequences of our actions, adhering to moral duties and obligations, and cultivating virtuous traits that can guide our behavior in challenging situations.

One of the key insights we have emphasized is the interplay between personal values and business ethics. We have encouraged readers to reflect on their own values and how they align with the ethical standards of the business world. By recognizing the influence of personal values on decision-making, individuals can make more informed choices that align with their own moral compass.

Additionally, we have delved into the role of ethical leadership in fostering an ethical culture within organizations. We have emphasized the importance of leaders setting a positive example, promoting transparency, and encouraging open communication. By doing so, leaders can inspire ethical behavior and create an environment where employees feel empowered to act ethically.

Furthermore, we have discussed the ethical implications of various business practices, such as sustainability, corporate social responsibility, and stakeholder management. We have stressed the need for businesses to go beyond profit maximization and consider the impact of their actions on the environment, society, and all stakeholders involved.

In conclusion, "Ethics in Action: Empowering Every Individual in Business" aims to equip individuals with the knowledge and tools necessary to make ethical decisions in the realm of business. By understanding key concepts and insights, readers can cultivate a strong ethical foundation and contribute to a more responsible and sustainable business world. Let us all remember that ethics is not just a niche field for experts; it is a collective responsibility that every individual in business should embrace.

The Ongoing Journey of Ethical Decision-Making

Ethics in Action: Empowering Every Individual in Business

Introduction:

In today's business landscape, ethical decision-making holds a paramount significance. It is not just a matter of complying with laws and regulations but also about fostering trust, integrity, and sustainability. Every individual, regardless of their role or position in an organization, has a moral responsibility to make ethical decisions. This subchapter explores the ongoing journey of ethical decision-making and provides practical insights to empower every individual in business.

Understanding the Nature of Ethical Decision-Making:

Ethical decision-making is a complex process that involves evaluating different options, considering the impact on stakeholders, and aligning actions with ethical principles. It requires a deep understanding of values, moral reasoning, and the ability to navigate ethical dilemmas. This subchapter delves into the various theoretical frameworks and models that can assist individuals in making ethical choices.

Developing Ethical Awareness:

To embark on the journey of ethical decision-making, individuals must first develop ethical awareness. This entails recognizing the ethical dimensions of situations, understanding personal biases and cultural influences, and embracing a commitment to act ethically. The subchapter provides practical exercises and real-life examples to enhance ethical awareness and encourage introspection.

Building Ethical Competence:

Ethical decision-making is a skill that can be honed through continuous learning and practice. It requires individuals to develop ethical competence by understanding the ethical codes and standards of their profession, engaging in ethical discussions, and seeking guidance when faced with complex ethical dilemmas. The subchapter offers strategies and resources to enhance ethical competence and encourages individuals to become ethical leaders in their organizations.

Navigating Ethical Challenges:

In the fast-paced and ever-changing business environment, individuals often encounter ethical challenges. Whether it is dealing with conflicts of interest, pressure to compromise values, or witnessing unethical behavior, individuals need tools and strategies to navigate these challenges. This subchapter provides practical tips and case studies to help individuals make ethical choices even in the face of adversity.

Conclusion:

Ethical decision-making is a continuous journey that requires ongoing commitment and effort. By understanding the nature of ethical decision-making, developing ethical awareness and competence, and navigating ethical challenges, every individual can contribute to a more ethical and sustainable business environment. This subchapter empowers every individual, regardless of their background or position, to embrace ethics in action and make a positive difference in the world of business.

Inspiring a Culture of Ethical Responsibility and Empowerment

In today's ever-evolving business landscape, the importance of ethics cannot be overstated. It is not enough for businesses to merely comply with legal standards; they must actively strive to create a culture of ethical responsibility and empowerment. This subchapter aims to shed light on the significance of ethical conduct in business and provide actionable strategies to inspire individuals at all levels to embrace ethical values and drive positive change.

Ethics in Action: Empowering Every Individual in Business is a book that addresses the pressing need for ethical responsibility in the corporate world. Its insights are applicable to every individual, whether they are business owners, employees, or consumers. By focusing on the niche of business ethics, this subchapter delves deeper into the challenges and opportunities that arise when ethical conduct becomes a fundamental aspect of a company's culture.

The subchapter starts by emphasizing the importance of ethical responsibility and its role in building trust, reputation, and long-term success. It highlights how ethical behavior not only benefits organizations but also impacts society as a whole. By inspiring readers to understand the significance of ethics in business, the subchapter aims to create a collective mindset that values integrity, transparency, and fairness.

Furthermore, the subchapter offers practical strategies to empower individuals within organizations to actively contribute to a culture of ethical responsibility. It explores the role of leadership in shaping ethical conduct and highlights the importance of clear communication, training, and accountability. By providing examples of companies that have successfully fostered an ethical environment, readers gain insights into how to implement ethical practices effectively.

Additionally, the subchapter addresses the empowerment aspect of ethical responsibility. It emphasizes the need to empower every individual, regardless of their position in the organizational hierarchy, to make ethical decisions and take responsibility for their actions. It explores the concept of ethical decision-making frameworks, providing readers with tools to navigate complex ethical dilemmas and make principled choices.

In conclusion, "Inspiring a Culture of Ethical Responsibility and Empowerment" is a subchapter that aims to engage a broad audience, including business owners, employees, and consumers. By highlighting the importance of ethics in business and providing actionable strategies, it empowers readers to drive positive change within their organizations and contribute to a more ethical and responsible business world.

Printed in the USA
CPSIA information can be obtained
at www.ICGtesting.com
CBHW071311200724
11858CB00023B/588